Manzil

Dhanu Prathap

BookLeaf Publishing

India | USA | UK

Presentation by *BookLeaf Publishing*

Web: www.bookleafpub.com

E-mail: info@bookleafpub.com

ISBN: 9789357447393

First edition 2022

To all the friends with beautiful souls who continue to give me unconditional love. I am truly blessed to have such wonderful gems in my life. Thank you!

Author's Note

I write poems
In hopes that my words
Have the strength
My voice never had...

Mother - Daughter Disconnect

"I held you in my womb for nine months."
Funny you say that,
for it was only after the cord was cut
that I took my first breath.
Why is it mother that you forget of this?

Love You A Latte

Hi there, can I have a Grande Caramel Latte
with a shot of espresso and oat milk?
Darling Dearest,
May your significant other be as specific as your
coffee order.

Lady At The Coffee Shop

Hm, she's waiting for someone
While brushing her tousled hair
Every movement seems to be in tandem with her
surroundings
The man behind her stands in awe
The child next to her smiles
But she only sees a text message.

The Untold Stories

Look into the graveyard
These are the stories
that need to be told.

The woman who never reunited
with her lover.

The dog who stayed by his owner
till his last breath.

The father who fought
to keep his family safe.

The boy who took his life
because of the pain.

The loyal mother who wanted
her children to always be happy.

The child who never took
her first steps.

Why remake a movie
With the same storyline
When there are so many
Other stories than can be told
For the first time?

Stay Strong,

5

A broken heart
Will seem like the worst has come.
A healed heart
Won't be one so easily undone.

Role Model

Look like her.
Love like her.
Sound like her.
Dress like her.
Read like her.
Speak like her.
Dance like her.
Smile like her.
Smell like her.
Eat like her.

When
I
look
in
the
mirror,
I
no
longer
see
me.
I see her.

Ties vs. Eyeliner

T: So much talk about feminism
E: And still you haven't changed.

T: You can never do a man's work
E: Yet it is being done.

T: Behind every great man is a successful
woman
E: So you cannot do things on your own.

T: You need a man in your life
E: We have different understandings of
essentials.

T: I have all the answers
E: But you never listened to my questions.

54321 Meditation

5

I see a baby fidgeting with her blanket
I see a mom trying to sort her day
I see young ballerinas prancing past the
Halloween decor
I see the barista confirming 15 orders
I see my screen still remains blank.

4

I feel the keys on my laptop
I feel my dry hands needing lotion
I feel bracelets moving back and forth on my
wrists
I feel my toes moving in my fuzzy shoes.

3

I hear my nails tapping on the table
I hear the barista yelling out completed orders
I hear the ballerinas squealing in delight.

2

I smell the coffee in the air
I smell the jasmine in my hair.

1

I taste old coffee on my tongue; it's time for
another sip.

Streaming with my First Love

So I picked a college major that was best for my future according to everyone, studied, and drank liquor of all different colors. You kept me in my best shape. I never did go to Taco Tuesday in fear it would compromise my ability to give you the best.

So I left the love of my life to go through with this arranged marriage with education.

I did try to forget you. But see, the problem is I saw you everywhere.

Music would play, and my mind immediately began to count the beats. Uh, one two three four would watch dancers and long to be back on the stage. I would watch practices in the car parking lots as I cut through to the library.

Suddenly choreographies were created in my mind. The waxed stage floors. The sound of the stage when I banged my feet in motion looking into the darkness where I could see the occasional audience member checking their phone.

I tried to focus on education with rigor, but every so often, my mind would drift back to you as tunes played while pages gliding underneath my fingertips.

The late nights on the basketball courts, praying for the lights to stay on for a bit longer so I could be with you knowing I was the happiest with you.

Nevertheless I was loyal to my education. It wasn't my love, wasn't the passion. I wrote, studied, and passed.

In the end, I received my degree, the greatest divorce I could have received, and finally told myself I was free.

Now I must be honest. I cannot say my education was a waste of time. This was a learning experience that was mine and mine only. I don't regret it because I did my best with the information I had then. But now, that's over, and my love for you has grown fonder.

Excitedly I ran back to you, hoping you would take me back. Forgive me for the time I spent away.

Instead, you made me work to have you back in my life. My bones forgot the way I used to move. My breaths would grow short. Now you cared more for others who put you first.

But you were my first love, and I couldn't bear to leave you ever again. So I worked! I sweated to the point where my body looked like I walked out of the shower. I smiled, seeing calluses form again. I danced with children, learned from the adults who stopped loving you, and I'll keep dancing until the day you take me back into your arms.

Mama's Cake Recipe

1/2 teaspoon of the tear mama wipes away as
her precious children walk into the room.

2 cups of mama's silence every time guests come
over.

3/4 cups of the strength mama has to listen
to the hurls of abuses papa throws.

One tablespoon of smile mama gets when we
choose to sit next to her.

Different from the Rest

Hey,
Today you were told that you look funny. It's
just the illiteracy of a young being who has
never seen anyone like you. In the land where
fast food joints were scattered across the roads,
your mama was making pappadams and dhaal.
It's okay to be mad. It's rude to make fun of
other people's differences. You experienced it
and know that it was wrong, but they learned
much later. I know when you look in the mirror,
you pin back that stray hair or cover the scars
you made against the mind that made you ticks.
But I promise survival has its glory and you too
will experience it. It's not going to be an easy
route to happiness, but you are in charge of
yourself and let no one else take that power from
you.
Sincerely,
An Older You

Forgive

As I look at the face in the mirror,
I see that an apology needs to be made.
I'm sorry for all that I've put you through
and most importantly I need to forgive you.
I spoke so harshly over these past years.
Anytime I made a mistake. I blamed you.
Why didn't you know better,
how could you make that choice,
what possessed you?
I'm sorry love, I really am.
So as I look into the mirror
staring back at those questioning eyes,
I smile,
because darling, there's so much you are meant
to do and become
and I accept you for all that you are -

Frankenstein

A product of love, yet the world sees only a
monster, who is known as the one who uses the
limbs of others to walk and destroy everything
in its path for a broken heart.

But isn't that what we all are?

Rather than taking the limbs of another, we take
the trauma of our ancestors, and we rage this
earth. Plundering through its resources taking for
ourselves, but never in a moment do we look at
you and think; you and I are one and the same.

Unbearable as it is to face ourselves, we look at
you dear Frankenstein and call you a monster.

Lone Wolves

The pain of being alone
when you have everyone

Is a pain that can
cut through steel-

It stems from where love is lost
Even a little light is
gripped onto for dear life

Every name, every face
becomes forgotten
when the darkness seeps in
The routine of smiling
making jokes
conversing with others
becomes habit
for it no longer comes
from a place of interest

The greatest actors
in the world are we
the ones who smile
in the crowds and
flip our pillows
to avoid the tears from the
night before...

The Story of The Poet

Pen and paper meet again, conducted by her
hands
Taking her time with each word

Today what shall she write about...
A broken heart
A wandering soul
Pains of the past

She rips her own heart apart
so that others may
find solace in her words

Rest in Peace

You stopped adding to our playlist
but I still play our songs on repeat
Without you, it seems
our music has lost its sound

It was painful to have been
building a palace of dreams
only to be left with
ruins of memories in its place…

As new memories begin to dance
You fade beyond my reach
Despite this,
I still protect you
As I put balm on my scars

My eyes search the night sky
As the stars smile back
Hoping my prayers reach you
When my words never could

For the ghosts of those
beautiful memories still,
put a smile on my face
and as the words I wrote
immortalize what once was

But truly it is finally time for
me to lay this matter to rest.

Bartender!

One shot to get me in the mood
Two shots to put on some moves
Three shots to have a fun night
Four shots to forget wrong and right
Five shots to follow in suit
Six shots to forget.

Focus is the Act of Working

9 pm. reads the clock
Time to begin
clickity-clack on my Mac

9:30 reads the clock
I need more time
clickity-clack on my Mac

9:42 reads the clock
I'll wait until 9:45
clickity-clack on my Mac

10:00 reads the clock
It's go-time
clickity-clack on my Mac

10:27 reads the clock
Time for a break
clickity-clack on my Mac

11 pm reads the clock
One hour on the clock time to edit away
clickity-clack on my Mac

11:59 reads the clock
A minute before time's up
clickity-clack on my Mac

Log Kya Kahenge

It is true that no one can walk the path we chose.
But what does one do?
When the voice of the mass
are those of family, friends, and loved ones.
As their voices turn too shrill
and even after they have left your side
you hear the voices of theirs
ringing with the words
that were once said.
For the old voices of distaste
will be replaced.
But keep on with the course you chose.
For your soul's calling deserves
more love than the ones who have
no faith.

Manzil

Emotions flowed as words
on to the page
Escaping from societal standards
and their expectations
I smiled cried and cursed
as I wrote away
Nights and days went by
as I lost the dates
Thank you for the love and hatred
Now I have my peace